CHANGING THE FACE OF POWER

Women in the U.S. Senate

Focus on American History Series

Center for American History   University of Texas at Austin

Edited by DON CARLETON

CHANGING THE

FACE OF POWER

Women in the U.S. Senate

Photographs by MELINA MARA

Foreword by COKIE ROBERTS   Introduction by SENATOR BARBARA MIKULSKI

Introduction by SENATOR KAY BAILEY HUTCHISON   Interviews by HELEN THOMAS

 UNIVERSITY OF TEXAS PRESS *Austin*

First edition, 2005

Appendices 1–3 copyright © Center for American Women and Politics 2005

Requests for permission to reproduce material from this work should be sent to:
Permissions
University of Texas Press
P.O. Box 7819
Austin, TX 78713-7819
www.utexas.edu/utpress/about/bpermission.html

⊗ The paper used in this book meets the minimum requirements
of ANSI/NISO Z39.48-1992 (R1997) (Permanence of Paper).

LIBRARY OF CONGRESS CATALOGING-IN-PUBLICATION DATA

Mara, Melina, 1962–
Changing the face of power : women in the U.S. Senate / photographs by Melina Mara ; foreword
by Cokie Roberts ; introduction by Senator Barbara Mikulski ; introduction by Senator Kay Bailey
Hutchison ; interviews by Helen Thomas.
    p.   cm. — (Focus on American history series)
 ISBN 0-292-70975-7 (hardcover : alk. paper)
    1. Women legislators—United States—Portraits.   2. Portrait photography—United States.   3. Mara,
Melina, 1962–   I. Title.   II. Series.
 TR681.L4M37 2005
 328.73'092'2—dc22
                                                                2005007628

Contents

Foreword

COKIE ROBERTS

IF you sit in the Gallery and look down, they stand out as splashes of color in a sea of blue-gray. For years, only one woman, then two, mingled with male colleagues in the Senate Chamber during the ritualistic calling of the roll. From above they looked like accents of red or yellow on a black-and-white photograph. Now, with fourteen women in the Senate, they transform the picture.

The transformation, of course, is not just one of appearance. The outcome of those roll calls changes when there's a critical mass of women in a legislature. The Center for American Women and Politics has compiled data over decades showing that lawmakers who are female put a higher priority on issues affecting women, children, and families than their male counterparts, and cross party lines to assure success. That's been a political fact at the state level for years. Finally, there are enough women in the United States Senate for it to be true at the national level as well.

And, these women report, their presence in the room where decisions are being made can have a sometimes-subtle impact. Their life experiences have been different from those of most of the men, and they bring those experiences to the table—whether it's as a mother of young children, the caretaker of an elderly parent, the widow who lost her credit, or the candidate who was shut out from the boardrooms where campaign funds are raised.

Melina Mara captures those differences in her wonderfully expressive series of photographs of the women who belong to what has been called the most exclusive club in America. Remarkably, these black-and-white renditions seem suffused with color, simply because the women stand out. The picture of feet—Maria Cantwell's stylish high heels in a circle of pedestrian men's lace-ups—reveals more than any words could convey.

Because the women of the Senate had sense enough to give the photographer remarkable access, the pictures take us into backrooms and even bathrooms. Mary Landrieu stops at the sink between meetings, quickly freshening her makeup, so she can put her best face forward. Elizabeth Dole, her usually well-coifed hair flying in the breeze, clutches her family Bible while riding the Senate subway with her husband, Bob, on the way to her swearing-in.

The pictures of a senator-mom make any mother smile in recognition. Blanche Lincoln, squatting to be on a level with her twin sons, is talking on the phone as they wait. You can tell that they won't wait for long. Kay Bailey Hutchison, walking with her eighteen-month-old daughter, is in no hurry to catch up with the mass of senators whose backs are to her, oblivious to the delightful little creature at their rear.

Perhaps most symbolic is a photograph of Lisa Murkowski framed by her office window, which instantly brings to mind the famous rendition of President Kennedy leaning over his desk, peering out with his back to us, alone with the burden of power. Senator Murkowski faces us, addressing her staff according to the caption, engaging others in her task, as these women say they do. The picture literally changes the face of power.

That's what these women do every day in the United States Senate. Here is their story.

Introduction

SENATOR BARBARA MIKULSKI

EACH of the women of the United States Senate has her own story of personal courage and achievement. Many of us didn't come to politics by the traditional route, for example, being in a nice law firm or belonging to the right clubs. Instead, we got involved because of a community need—that's what happened to me.

I believe in "operationalizing your good intentions." As a young social worker, I fought a highway that was going to destroy Baltimore communities, including the East Baltimore neighborhood of Highlandtown where I grew up. This highway would have sliced neighborhoods in half and destroyed the homes of people trying to live the American dream. I used principles of community organizing to fight this road, the same skills I use today in the Senate.

Before I came to the Senate in 1986, in all of American history only fifteen women had served in the United States Senate; one served only a single day. I was the first Democratic woman elected in her own right, and I knew that put me at an initial disadvantage. It wasn't just that the gym was off-limits. I didn't have any natural mentors to show me the ropes.

I knew I didn't want to be one of the boys, but I did want to be one of the gang. So I did two things. First, I asked for help. I established a relationship with the old guard and asked for advice. I was respectful of them, and respected the rules of the Senate. Second, I did my homework. I went to all of the hearings and showed up on time. I read all of the reports, traveled with the other senators on fact-finding trips, studied the issues, and became known as reliable. Because I worked hard and formed alliances, I was rewarded with powerful committee assignments and the respect of my colleagues.

Though I was the first, I didn't want to be the first and only. I wanted to be the first of many. When four women joined me in the Senate in 1993, I was so proud. It would not be every woman for herself in the Senate. I proudly took on the role of mentor and adviser.

I organized a workshop for my new colleagues, so I could teach them the inner workings of the Senate, explain how to organize their new offices, and show them how to get on the best committees. I shared with them the organizing principles I use to guide my office—things like "We cannot always guarantee an outcome, but we can guarantee an effort" and "Our constituents have a right to know, to be heard, and to be represented." I wanted to open some of the doors that had been opened for me, and make sure that the new women in the Senate would be successful.

When my Republican colleague Senator Kay Bailey Hutchison joined the U.S. Senate, we were determined that bipartisan civility would begin with us. Now, at the start of every Senate, I hold a bipartisan power workshop for all the women of the Senate. We started the tradition of monthly dinner meetings for all the women senators to build friendship and fellowship; we have been through adoptions, showers, and weddings and have built common ground.

I'm so proud that the women of the Senate work together, act as role models and mentors for other women, and make a difference by standing up for a variety of issues important to women and families. Together, we are opening doors for the next generation of leadership.

Introduction

SENATOR KAY BAILEY HUTCHISON

WHEN I first looked at Melina Mara's photograph of my daughter, Bailey, walking with me, I was stunned by the impact of that simple black-and-white image. Melina captured a private moment and made it a powerful statement about the changing nature of leadership and representation in our country. This scene—a mother leading her toddler daughter toward a sea of men in dark suits—could never have been possible in the past. The daughter has wandered away from the event, unconcerned about its importance, focused solely on emulating her mother's steps— unaware that the steps are breaking barriers for her.

The photos in this book are an amazing compilation that display a modern and seldom seen side of the United States Senate. The images of the fourteen female senators tell a quiet story of strength, hard work, and perseverance. The intimate way in which the collection chronicles the revolving roles of legislator, mother, and leader provides a snapshot of the unique life of a woman in the Senate, and puts on the image of the Senate a different face, a different pair of shoes, a new perspective.

The Senate is a staid, formal institution sometimes billed as the "greatest deliberative body in the world." It's not known for its well-developed sense of humor or for adapting quickly to change. Though the serious nature of our business remains, the vitality and diversity that women have brought have contributed greatly to the chamber and, more importantly, to society at large.

Melina is owed a debt of gratitude for capturing these remarkable images. Depicted in black, white, and shades of gray, our day-to-day lives on Capitol Hill tell more than just personal stories. They foretell change. Melina worked tirelessly and creatively to sense the interesting moments and record them without our noticing she was there. I never even saw her the day she took the cover picture.

The collection indeed shows the changing face of influence—it is a face that looks much like the one seen in the mirror by half of the United States population. These images symbolize the way in which our nation is becoming a place where each child—boy or girl—has a real and equal opportunity to succeed.

When Bailey grows up, it is my hope she won't see our picture as symbolic at all. She'll think of it as a sweet moment captured by a photograph.

CHANGING THE FACE OF POWER

Women in the U.S. Senate

Photographs BY MELINA MARA

Senator Dianne Feinstein (D-CA) speaks to a fellow senator on the telephone as two of her staffers converse in the foreground. Feinstein began her political career in 1970 with her election to the San Francisco Board of Supervisors; she served as San Francisco's mayor in 1978–1989, ran unsuccessfully for California governor in 1990, and won election to the Senate in 1992. (February 2003)

After casting her vote concerning an amendment to the education bill, Senator Blanche Lincoln (D-AR) runs off the Senate floor to keep an appointment. Practicing a bipartisan style of governing, Lincoln works with her colleagues on such issues as taxes, the environment, education, health care, and agriculture. Lincoln has a rural background, being from a seventh-generation Arkansas farm family. (May 2001)

Senior Senator Olympia Snowe (R-ME) listens along with her male colleagues to testimony on intelligence matters during Select Committee on Intelligence hearing in the Dirksen Senate Office Building on Capitol Hill. Snowe has three other committee assignments: Committee on Commerce, Science and Education; Committee on Finance; and Committee on Small Business and Entrepreneurship, which she chairs. (February 2003)

Senator Mary Landrieu (D-LA) greets friends and constituents before speaking at an Acts of Caring Awards Ceremony on Capitol Hill. Landrieu held office in the Louisiana House from 1980 to 1988, was the state's treasurer from 1988 to 1996, and was a candidate for governor in 1995. Landrieu is one of four women senators with young children. (April 2001)

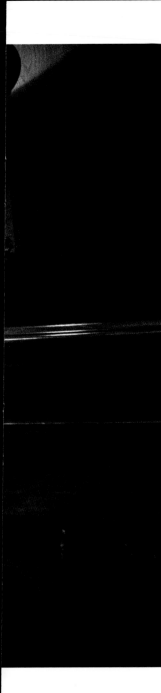

Under the watchful eye of a TV camera, Senator Hillary Rodham Clinton (D-NY) peers over the massive wooden desk before asking questions of Environmental Protection Agency Administrator Christine Todd Whitman during the Environment and Natural Resources Committee hearing on arsenic levels in drinking water, held in the Russell Senate Office Building on Capitol Hill. Entering the Senate as a former First Lady, Clinton initially won praise for keeping a low profile upon taking office. (May 2001)

After a press conference introducing legislation to allow widows of veterans who choose to remarry after the age of fifty-five to continue receiving benefits, senior Senator Kay Bailey Hutchison (R-TX), left, and Senator Hillary Rodham Clinton (D-NY), rear center, speak to widows denied those benefits under current law. Women in Congress and at the state legislative level have a long history of working across the aisle around common interests. (January 2003)

After casting her vote, Senator Barbara Boxer (D-CA) listens to questions from reporters off the Senate floor on Capitol Hill. A Capitol Police officer stands, left. (April 2001)

Freshman Senator Elizabeth Dole (R-NC) rides the Senate train with her husband, former Senator Bob Dole, on their way to her swearing-in ceremony on the Senate floor in the Capitol. Elizabeth Dole, a former transportation secretary and presidential candidate, carries a family Bible to be used during the ceremony. The underground train connects the Senate offices with the Capitol. (January 2003)

Senator Barbara Boxer (D-CA) stands on a footstool, dubbed the "Boxer Box," to boost her height as she speaks to Californians visiting the Capitol. Boxer discussed the economy and the impending war with Iraq before posing for pictures with each constituent in a meeting room at the Dirksen Senate Office Building. (February 2003)

After casting her vote concerning the education bill,
Senior Senator Patty Murray (D-WA) talks with Senator
John D. Rockefeller IV (D-WV), left, while waiting for
the "Senators Only" elevator off the Senate floor. The
original "mom in tennis shoes" candidate, Murray
is known for supporting education, transportation,
employment opportunities, and workers. (March 2001)

Senator Dianne Feinstein (D-CA) is embraced by
Senator Patrick J. Leahy (D-VT), left, before an Amber
Alert press conference outside the doors of the Senate
Radio and TV Gallery in the Capitol. Senator Orrin G.
Hatch (R-UT), is at right. In a bipartisan effort, Senator
Kay Bailey Hutchison and Senator Feinstein sponsored
the National Amber Network Act, which the Senate
unanimously passed twice.

The Amber Alert system is a partnership between
law-enforcement agencies and broadcasters to activate
an urgent bulletin in certain child-abduction cases.
(January 2003)

History and tradition are seen everywhere on Capitol Hill. Senator Susan Collins (R-ME) has a meeting off the Senate floor in the Senate Reception Room—a room filled with frescos and portraits of past senators. (October 2003)

Senator Kay Bailey Hutchison (R-TX) chairs the
Aviation Subcommittee of the Committee on Commerce,
Science, and Transportation in the Russell Senate
Office Building on Capitol Hill. In the 108th Congress,
Hutchison is vice chair of the Senate Republican
Conference. (April 2001)

Arkansas' Democratic freshman senator, Blanche
Lincoln, gives thumbs up to Senator Barbara Boxer
(D-CA) during a reception on Capitol Hill for a
Public Broadcasting Services program entitled To the
Contrary. Launched in April 1992, To the Contrary,
an all-female news analysis series, is celebrating its
tenth season on the air. (April 2001)

*After a long committee meeting on Capitol Hill,
Senator Mary Landrieu (D-LA) stops by the women's
restroom in the Dirksen Senate Office Building.
Landrieu serves on Appropriations, Energy and
Natural Resources, and Small Business and
Entrepreneurship committees. (April 2001)*

Overeager supporters try to help newly elected Senator Elizabeth Dole (R-NC) down from the stage during an evening celebration at the Chamber of Commerce Building that followed her swearing-in ceremony as a U.S. senator. The sixty-six-year-old Dole had to pull away from the crowd's grip and insist on finding a safer route to the floor. (January 2003)

Senator Barbara Boxer (D-CA) listens to testimony concerning the future of Iraq during a Committee on Foreign Relations hearing in the Dirksen Senate Office Building on Capitol Hill. After serving for ten years in the House of Representatives, Boxer became a United States senator in January 1993. Some of her primary issues are education, environmental protection, abortion rights, and human rights. (February 2003)

Senator Lisa Murkowski (R-AK) speaks to a fellow freshman senator, Jim Talent (R-MO), during President George W. Bush's State of the Union speech on the House floor on Capitol Hill. Only 14 percent of the seats in the U.S. Congress are held by women. (January 2003)

In a small conference room, Senator Jean Carnahan (D-MO) and former New Jersey Senator Bill Bradley participate in a phone interview during a campaign stop at Barnes Jewish Hospital in St. Louis. The interview with a local radio station focused on health care, the subject of a press conference held later at the hospital. Bradley joined Carnahan during several stops of her campaign to win the Senate seat for a full term. (October 2002)

Senator Kay Bailey Hutchison (R-TX) looks over papers just moments before a joint press conference with Senator Hillary Rodham Clinton (D-NY) in a bipartisan effort to introduce legislation to allow widows of veterans who choose to remarry after the age of fifty-five to continue receiving benefits. Hutchison serves on the Committee on Commerce, Science, and Transportation; Committee on Appropriations; Committee on Rules and Administration; and Committee on Veterans Affairs. (January 2003)

Senator Susan Collins (R-ME) speaks during a press conference at the Senate Radio and TV Gallery on Capitol Hill, taking a bipartisan stand with Senator Charles Schumer (D-NY) in support of changes to President Bush's energy plan. A centrist, Collins frequently seeks compromises with Democrats and forms bipartisan alliances to get results. During the 108th Congress, Collins chairs the Governmental Affairs Committee; she is only the third woman in history to chair a full-standing committee. (May 2001)

First-term Senator Maria Cantwell (D-WA) pauses outside a hearing room to take questions from reporters in the Dirksen Senate Office Building on Capitol Hill. Cantwell, a high-tech millionaire, worked as a marketing executive of Real Networks, a Seattle Internet audio software company, before running for her Senate seat. Cantwell previously served in the Washington state House from 1987 to 1992 and won election to the U.S. House in 1993 but was defeated for re-election in 1994. (February 2003)

At an evening reception for former Texas Senator Lloyd Bentsen on Capitol Hill, freshman Senator Hillary Rodham Clinton (D-NY) has a private word. In the doorway stands one of the members of the Secret Service who accompany the former First Lady. As a first-term senator, Clinton is seen by her supporters as a policy innovator who is becoming more and more active in her party's leadership structure. Clinton is the only First Lady ever to win election to a federal office. (May 2001)

Freshman Senator Maria Cantwell (D-WA), center, jokes with fellow Washington state Senator Patty Murray (D-WA) and Senator Debbie Stabenow (D-MI) while riding the "Senators Only" elevator on their way to a vote on campaign-finance reform. Washington is one of three states where both Senate seats are held by women. California and Maine are the other two. (April 2001)

Freshman Senator Lisa Murkowski (R-AK) speaks to her staffers before a meeting on Capitol Hill with senior Alaska Senator Ted Stevens (R-AK). Before coming to the Senate, Murkowski, a lawyer, served three terms in the Alaska House of Representatives. She is a member of the Energy and Natural Resources Committee, Environment and Public Works Committee, Veterans Affairs Committee, and Indian Affairs Committee. (March 2003)

Senator Maria Cantwell (D-WA) meets with members of her staff at her office on Capitol Hill moments before leaving to cast a vote on the Senate floor. Cantwell's committee positions are Energy and Natural Resources, Indian Affairs, Commerce, and Small Business and Entrepreneurship. (March 2001)

With her children's pictures crowding her desk, Senator Debbie Stabenow (D-MI), listens to a staff member during a meeting in her office on Capitol Hill. In the Senate and throughout her political career, Stabenow's primary issues have included health care, prescription drugs, education, the environment, and working with the business community in Michigan. (May 2001)

Senator Blanche Lincoln (D-AR) signs papers while sandwiched between her twin sons, Reece and Bennett, at a Get Caught Reading event led by former Representative Pat Schroeder (D-CO) on Capitol Hill. Lincoln, elected in 1998, is the youngest woman ever elected to the United States Senate and the second woman in Arkansas—Hattie Caraway in 1932 being the first—to be elected to the office. Lincoln is one of four women senators with young children. (May 2001)

Being a senator means constantly shuttling to and from the home state. With one of the Senate's longest commutes, Republican Senator Lisa Murkowski from Alaska works while flying home on an early morning flight. (October 2003)

Senator Barbara Boxer (D-CA) confers with Senator
Joseph Biden (D-DE), vice-chairman and Democratic
ranking member, before a Committee on Foreign
Relations hearing in the Russell Senate Office Building
on Capitol Hill, where Secretary of State Colin
Powell is about to address issues concerning Iraq,
North Korea, and the war on terrorism. Boxer's other
committee assignments are Commerce, Science and
Transportation, and Environment and Public Works.
(February 2003)

*On Capitol Hill, Senator Barbara Mikulski (D-MD)
stands with fellow female senators Hillary Rodham
Clinton (D-NY), center, and Barbara Boxer (D-CA),
left, during a press conference at the Senate Radio
and TV Gallery on the anniversary of the* Roe vs.
Wade *Supreme Court decision. Mikulski is an ardent
supporter of abortion rights. She is the longest-serving
woman now in the U.S. Senate, having entered in
1987, and is affectionately called "dean" of the women
senators. (January 2003)*

Senator Maria Cantwell (D-WA) kids with reporters from Washington state during an informal on-the-record interview in her Capitol Hill office. During this meeting, Cantwell discussed energy issues and Washington state's economic climate. (January 2003)

*Senior Senator Olympia Snowe (R-ME) speaks to
her press secretary, Dave Lackey, in a stairwell
off the Senate floor prior to a vote. With Snowe's
election to the Senate in 1994, she became only
the second woman senator in history to represent
Maine, following the late Senator Margaret Chase
Smith, who served from 1949 to 1973. Snowe focuses
on a number of issues, such as budget and fiscal
responsibility; education, including student financial
aid and education technology; national security;
women's issues; health care; and campaign finance
reform. (March 2003)*

Senior Senator Patty Murray (D-WA) leaves her office on Capitol Hill, followed by her chief of staff, Rick Desimone, after a staff meeting. Growing in prominence in her party, Murray was chosen in 2002 to head the Democratic Senatorial Campaign Committee, raising a record $129 million. She was the first woman ever to hold that position. (March 2001)

Hoping for an interview, reporters wait for senators as they exit the Senate floor after a vote. Senator Dianne Feinstein (D-CA) answers the questions of reporters while waiting for the "Senators Only" elevator off the Senate floor. (October 2003)

*After a meeting with members of the Arkansas
Chamber of Commerce who are visiting Washington,
D.C., Senator Blanche Lincoln (D-AR) acknowledges
a friend at the close of the gathering at the Dirksen
Senate Office Building on Capitol Hill. Lincoln comes
from a seven-generation farm family. (May 2001)*

Before beginning a conversation, Senator Edward Kennedy (D-MA) places his hand on the shoulder of Senator Patty Murray (D-WA) while waiting for the Women's Outreach meeting hosted by Senator John F. Kerry (D-MA) to begin on Capitol Hill. Democratic senators invited the leaders of various national women's organizations to discuss issues the groups care about, specifically how the current budget and tax debate could impact women. (March 2001)

Senator Lisa Murkowski (R-AK) meets on Capitol Hill with Senator John Cornyn (R-TX) to discuss the Arctic National Wildlife Refuge (ANWR). Senator Murkowski was appointed to the Senate post by her father, former Senator Frank H. Murkowski, who is now governor of Alaska. Like her father, Murkowski favors drilling for oil in the ANWR. (March 2003)

*Constituents from Missouri offer condolences
to Senator Jean Carnahan (D-MO), who lost her
husband, Mel Carnahan, and son, Roger, in a plane
crash. Governor Mel Carnahan died two weeks
before he was elected to the U.S. Senate, and Jean
Carnahan, one of her husband's closest advisers,
filled his Senate seat for two years before she was
defeated in the 2002 election. (April 2001)*

Senator Kay Bailey Hutchison, (R-TX), leads her daughter, Bailey, by the hand back to a line of fellow senators on the steps of the U.S. Capitol during a ceremony to remember the terrorist attacks on September 11, 2001. Hutchison always has one of her two children with her during the week while in Washington, D.C.; the family reunites each weekend in Texas. Her husband, Ray Hutchison, cares for their other child in Texas. Hutchison is one of the four women senators who have young children. (September 2002)

Interviews

BY HELEN THOMAS

I am Helen Thomas, a White House reporter.

I conducted face-to-face interviews with the fourteen U.S. women senators during the spring of 2003 and winter of 2004.

In these interviews, you will read answers to specifically pro forma questions which the senators answer with honesty and candor.

The senators speak about lifestyle changes, maintaining balance, male colleagues' treatment of women lawmakers, differences in governing styles, the possibility of a woman president on the horizon, the effectiveness of bipartisan teamwork, and much more.

Enjoy. And I hope you come away with a better understanding of women in politics.

Senator *Barbara Mikulski*
DEMOCRAT FROM MARYLAND

HT: *Do a lot of people come with women's issues, since you are a woman?*

BM: Well, you know, we come to the Senate representing our states. But we the women now feel, particularly with all fourteen of us, that every issue is a woman's issue, and we want to be sure that while the guys talk about the macro picture, we are talking about the macaroni and cheese issues whether it is here or around the world.

Have you seen any change in the attitudes towards the women senators?

We the women of the Senate experience what women who enter all nontraditional fields have faced. We broke glass ceilings; we battered down doors. But everyone knows that we are here to stay.

And just as the workplace has changed in the private sector, it has certainly changed here in the Senate.

Fourteen of us, representing everyone from a young dot-com executive who got started trying to save a library in her community like Maria Cantwell to a former First Lady like Senator Hillary Rodham Clinton, to a former head of the Red Cross and cabinetperson like Senator Dole, to me, a scrappy social worker who fought to save Baltimore's neighborhoods.

And will there be a lot more women senators, do you think?

I believe that every year we add more women to the United States Senate. And why? Because really we have a farm team of people who run for statewide office. There are women who are mayors, who are governors now, as well as come from the House of Representatives. So when I started in politics over two decades ago, we were just breaking in, whether it was in city council or state legislature. Then we went on to become members of Congress. When I first came to the Senate, I was the first Democratic woman to serve in both the House and the Senate. Now we have Senator Snowe and Senator Boxer and others who have done the same. And I anticipate more.

And are you really able to have a private life? Do things you really want to do? Kick off your shoes?

We really put in three shifts. We put in one shift being in the Senate. We put in another shift with our families and our friends, and a third shift being in our states with our constituents. And I have a little saying: I wish I were as thin as I am stretched.

Is there one highlight in your life that really moved you into politics?

When I was growing up as a young girl in the fifties, I never thought about politics. Politics in my neighborhood was boss machine politics. It was older, white, pot-bellied guys who smoked cigars. That wasn't for me, so I went into social work. But on my way to getting a doctorate, they were going to put a highway through Baltimore and take the older, ethnic neighborhoods. And I led the fight, because we couldn't get the doors of city hall opened. And I just knocked them down and went into politics. So now I see myself as a social worker with power.

Senator *Dianne Feinstein*

DEMOCRAT FROM CALIFORNIA

DF: I've been raised on constituent service, so I can't tell whether it has to do with my being a woman or not. But I very much believe that people often feel so far removed from their government—and that their government won't help them—that when they get an able response to an inquiry or when they have people that are willing to help them . . .

We help people with immigration problems, with social security problems, with veterans' problems—and we do this regardless of whether they're male or female.

HT: Have you noticed any difference in the way the male senators treat you? I mean, in the old days, just patronizing on the part of men? Or do you think you have total equality?

I think there are still vestigial remnants of the old boys' club. That still exists, but I think it is decreasing. I think the men are increasingly sensitized.

Are you optimistic about the future of women in the Senate—more women coming in?

I think from the get-go the woman has a better chance—if—if—she has done her apprenticeship—or as I say, earned her spurs. I think it's very difficult for a woman with no background in this arena to run for the Senate and make it. You have to have served in some capacity to understand the arena. Because what the voter is interested in, bottom line, is the effectiveness of the individual. If I vote for her, is she going to be an effective United States senator?

Do you think the presence of women in the Senate makes it more likely that women will participate in the political process? I think you do feel that way.

Yes. I remember when I was very young and I was running for governor, and I went to a Young Presidents' Organization wives' meeting. And I made my speech and they seemed to like what I said. And some came over afterwards, and they said, "What can we do to help?" And I said, knowing that they were the wives of presidents of major businesses—I said, "If you could contribute to me, I would really appreciate it." To a person, they said, "We have to go home and talk with our husbands about it." Today, that would not happen.

Is that right?

There is a change. Women now contribute on their own.

Can the people of America expect any of the women in the Senate to run for the presidency?

Oh, I think they can. Absolutely.

Do you have any ambition—in that direction?

Well . . . Do I have ambition in that direction? Um . . .

Say yes!
Do I believe I could be president? Yes.
Atta girl!
I think it is still very difficult for a woman to be in the highest executive office. I think as women get up around 20–25 percent of the Senate, the prognosis for a woman being president really doubles.
Would you run?
Yeah, I would run.
And how do you think a husband would handle a woman president? I guess it is just the same as a woman senator, right?
I've found the important thing for a busy woman in a high-profile job, with respect to her marriage, is to have a husband who is secure in who he is and what he does. And it really doesn't matter what he does, as long as he feels secure and is not threatened by what the woman does. And can actually enjoy it, rather than feel that it is kind of a putdown of him.
What strategies do you use to balance your private and public life?
My strategy is that family comes first. That if I can arrange a dinner with my family, that will come before virtually anything else.

One last question, which is: What impressions would you like the people who visit this women's exhibit to take away with them?
That women are capable. That we can be effective. That we are good legislative craftsmen. That we understand opportunity and timing as well as any man. That we have the drive, the staying power, and the motivation to do a job—and that our performance can be equal, if not better.

Senator Kay Bailey Hutchison
REPUBLICAN FROM TEXAS

HT: Do you think that women have made any change in the way the Senate operates?

KBH: When we come together on an issue, we win. Our colleagues know that if we are all together on an issue, they will want to be with us. And that comes out particularly in health-care issues—where we came out for mammograms being covered by insurance after the age of forty and we won. And for standards for mammograms. And I think that the more of us that come in, the more we will try to build consensus and stop the partisanship.

How optimistic are you about the future of women being elected? Do you think that there will be more?

I do. I think when you look at the success rate that women candidates have had . . . in the last two cycles, we've had about a 98 percent win rate.

The cycle before last, every candidate in the general election won. Everyone. Now the last session, we lost one but we gained two. So I think that we are going to see more women, because we now have the same credentials. In the old days, women would run from the school board or just a civic activist position—which is credible—but it would be hard to have name identification and the experience that people would look for. But now, women are running as congressmen, as state office holders, and they have had the experience and they are really accomplished and credible.

Do you find that in terms of your personal image, you have to adhere to certain protocol on your hair, your dress, your style?

Yes. I think that people expect you to look appropriate and professional. But they don't focus on it as much. When I first ran—when I was running for the legislature in the seventies—golly! People would really be judgmental. And if you did anything that they thought was inappropriate—your skirt was too short or your hair was too long—that would be a factor. Now I don't think it is a factor nearly as much.

What do you like about being a senator and what are the challenges? What are the frustrations?

What I like is the ability to make a difference in so many areas: making a difference in our national defense, our military priorities, our health care for women, education. I feel privileged to be a United States senator. But the downside is that you never control your schedule. If you controlled your time, you would be able to have normal meetings. But you can't, because you have a committee meeting called the day before, so that disrupts your schedule. Or you have votes. And then you have a commitment at home and you have to stay here and vote because you didn't finish your business, and so you disappoint people at home. That's the hard part.

Senator Debbie Stabenow

DEMOCRAT FROM MICHIGAN

DS: I actually started in local government—in county government back in the seventies—and have found myself really in part of the wave, I believe, of women coming into office. I was in local government in the seventies, state legislature in the eighties, the state senate and then the Congress in the nineties.

I have found myself, really, as women move each step. So always, there is an interest by the women in Michigan and across the country in my story and the stories of my colleagues. And they certainly want to hear from us.

I think one of the biggest struggles for women both as . . . as professionals is not to be stereotypes.

I remember in the county commission being on the Human Resources Committee, and the folks with child nutrition came to testify on the budget, and the chair of the committee turned to me and said, "Well that's your issue, Debbie." And I said, "Well you know, child nutrition is something that we all should care about. Moms and dads."

HT: *So there is a woman's impact per se?*
I think so. We all come with a different leadership style. Less about whose name is on an amendment, more about getting things done.

I think we have come a long way. I truly do think that we have come a long way, certainly, from when I started over twenty years ago. But the difficulty is when we get into issues—like now—such as war, foreign policy, armed services. We have women who are extremely knowledgeable on those committees. And I do not believe that they get their due in terms of the knowledge and expertise. And that's where I see a difference.

Do they get a voice?
They have a voice in that they are certainly able to speak at committee, speak at caucus, and so on.

But one of the concerns I have is [our] relationship to the media, quite frankly. When 9/11 happened, Mary Landrieu chaired a subcommittee related to terrorism, and I never saw her once being interviewed. Barbara Mikulski on the Intelligence Committee, I didn't see her once. Dianne Feinstein has tremendous credentials and expertise in our foreign affairs, and rarely did I see her. And so I . . . that . . . for me . . . One thing, for me—what I am still very frustrated about is the expertise of women, particularly on issues that are viewed as nontraditional. And I think that's when we have a problem—we're not hearing women.

Do you think any woman will run for president in the near future?

I do. I think that in just a few short years we'll have women that will be running as president and vice president.

Are there drawbacks to women who would even be considering it? Money? And the whole pressure on the families and the personal impact?

First of all, money is an issue. And being able to communicate your message means being able to buy time on television and radio—and that is a huge amount of money.

I think the first time that a woman runs on a major ticket—particularly one who wins a primary and goes on then to be the contender from either party—she will have extra pressures, will have a higher standard to meet. I think it is bound to be a situation where a lot of critical questions will be asked. And probably a lot of stereotypes will have to be eliminated in order for her to move forward.

But it is going to happen.

You think it will be tougher?

I think it will inherently be tougher. I do. I think it is very possible.

I think the first time a woman is the nominee of a major party, she may not be successful. If not, the second time we'll have someone who is successful, because I think it is going to happen sooner rather than later.

Senator *Hillary Rodham Clinton*

DEMOCRAT FROM NEW YORK

HT: *Your predecessors were approached by women because they were women in the Senate and very unique. Do you get that a lot now? In terms of women's issues?*

HRC: Well, I do get some of it, Helen, but I think that the numbers of women are now growing, so that we are not seen as unique or tokens. We're seen first as senators. And maybe second as women senators.

I think the changes in the last ten years have been dramatic. I mean, Barbara Mikulski—when she got here, there was no ladies' restroom. You could not wear pants on the floor of the Senate as a woman. So we have really seen a lot of both stylistic and substantive changes, I think.

Do you think the presence of women in the Senate makes it more likely that more women will participate in the political process?

I hope so. Certainly, more women have been willing to run, and I think women at all levels of government are encouraging individual women to be willing to participate. We still don't have a high enough participation of women as voters. And we still don't have the numbers that are anywhere near our population percentage—but we are making progress.

Do you meet with the other women senators for those monthly dinners?

I do, I do. I've had one at my home and I try to attend them every chance I can.

And do you talk about everything under the sun?

We talk about a lot of things. We talk about the very important issues that we are facing. We talk about personal matters. We talk about hints to survive—like what kinds of shoes to wear on these hard marble floors or where's the perfect pocketbook or attaché that carries everything. You know. We talk about all of those little hints.

And what is the toughest job about being a Senator?

That you have no control over your schedule. It is so difficult. You set your time and then a committee is called or a briefing from the Defense Department or a vote.

So you are constantly throughout the day finding that your time is not your own. When I say I am going to do something with my family or my friends, I just try every way I can to just do it. But you just try to keep that time as carefully protected as you can.

Is every social occasion a work obligation, or do you have a social life where you can just relax?

You know, most of them have elements of work involved. Because when you go out to dinner—either in New York or Washington—invariably somebody is going to come over and have something they want to talk about. It becomes difficult to separate out the social from the professional. But I really don't mind, because I know it is not often that everybody gets to see their senator.

When do you get to work in the morning?

It depends on what is going on. It depends. Some days early. Some days I don't have to be here quite so early. Every day is different. Every day is different.

And you go home when the day is done?

When the day is done, I get to go home.

Senator *Barbara Boxer*

DEMOCRAT FROM CALIFORNIA

BB: When I was elected to the House of Representatives—I took my seat in 1983—there were very few women in the House at that time. And I felt very much that I had a burden to bear, which was to really look out for the women all over the country, because there were so few of us out of 435. When I came over to the Senate, there were only two women in the United States Senate at that time.

HT: Is that right?

It was Barbara Mikulski and Nancy Kassebaum. So clearly, we also felt this obligation to reach beyond our states. Now for Senator Feinstein and myself coming at the same time, we made history—we were the first two women ever to represent one state in the United States Senate.

But I have to say the burden is far less now. Because if I look, for example, at the California congressional delegation, it's majority women that are the Democrats. There are more than twenty, and that's a huge number of women.

Why do you think that is?

I think the reason there are more women in the House and Senate is because we are doing a good job. And we never said we were better—we said we were equal. And I think that is clear. We are definitely equal and if I might say, perhaps in some cases, work a little harder because we still have to prove ourselves. And people are smart. They want the best that they can get for their vote.

Do you think they patronize you at all or treat you any differently? I mean, do they still have this different approach to women?

I have to say, in the United States Senate you are treated as an equal. And the reason, really, is not because everyone is so wonderful here—some are and some aren't—but one senator can really shut down this place. Those are the rules of the Senate. The House is very different. In the House, I found a lot more prejudice against women. We were considered kind of cute and new—and what were we about? And we could never get anywhere. We could never get to committee chairs.

They weren't being unkind—but you were a woman and that's the way they treated you?

In those years—I think they were being unkind. They didn't. They thought they were being gentlemanly and sweet. But now, when you look out at what I call the training ground—the local government, the state government, the state houses, the attorney generals' offices, the House of Representatives—what do you see? You're seeing women really taking hold.

This is a very natural profession for women. This

is a profession in many ways that is a nurturing profession, because you get to help so many people—whether it is fighting for people who do not have a voice—for little children or for victims of crime. This is a position where you can protect people. You know, after 9/11 my focus has been—just like it is on my family—to protect them, to protect my constituents.

And it is sort of a natural thing for women to want to do this. And I feel it is a profession that eventually—there will be—50 percent of the Senate will be women. I believe that.

How about a woman president? And would you run?
I would not run myself for president. I am just very happy doing the work I am doing. But there is no question in my mind—no doubt in my mind—there will be a woman president. And I think it will be sooner rather than later.

In the first quarter of the century?
Yes. I think it will be within the next fifteen years.

Do you have anyone in mind?
I do. I do. I really do. I mean, I am very willing to say that I think that Senator Hillary Clinton has what it takes to go the distance. I know it when I see it.

What it takes is sheer grit.
The ability to take a punch. It's a reason that it has taken women a little while to understand that. I only lost one race—my first race.

It was 1972. I was a very young woman then, with two young children. I ran for the local county board of supervisors and I lost that race. And what I learned after I lost the race was that it really takes a tremendous amount of self-respect and security to take a loss and the courage to do it the second time. And that was the hardest thing.

There was an article in *Ms.* magazine in the early seventies: The biggest problem with women? They couldn't come back after they lost. Women took it more personally. Now I think we are learning to take the punches.

Senator *Elizabeth Dole*

REPUBLICAN FROM NORTH CAROLINA

HT: Of all the jobs you've had—the White House, the FTC, the two cabinet, and then Red Cross—of all of those jobs, which did you enjoy the most? And senator, of course.

ED: Oh, I've loved them all. I really loved them all. Because each was completely different from the next but had its own set of important issues. And to me the goal has always been to try to—you know, public service is a way to give back for all of the blessings that we have in this country. It's kind of like a mission field. You know, you find those areas that are crying out for change. And of course, here in Washington, Union Station was my baby and so was National Airport. I loved working on those. And I remember Bob saying, "Forget trying to get the airports out of the federal government. It's been tried eight times since 1948 and never made it out of committee any of those eight times." And this was pillow talk. And he turned over and went to sleep. He said, "Forget it. It can't be done!"

And of course, then, that was throwing down the gauntlet! We were going to figure out how to do it. So when we did get it done three years later, and then especially when it was dedicated and we had the ceremony, I told that story. And told that story. And made a little fun of Bob, but he handled it fine. I said, "My husband said it couldn't be done."

But it was. In terms of your social life, do you feel that when you go out, you really have to be on? That you really have to be the senator?

No. Bob and I both feel that the two careers have enriched our marriage. And we both take great joy in what the other is doing. You don't get a lot of time to discuss it. It's like two ships passing in the night a lot. But you know, we're not social butterflies.

You're able to separate your private life and your public life?

Yes. In fact when we are home, we like to close that door and we like to watch *Law and Order* on television—or a good old movie on TNT or one of these classics—and just putter around the kitchen. We're not out on the social circuit.

What would you like people to take away from this exhibition?

I think the women who are in public service want to do everything they can to help other women reach their own potential. And we started an organization twenty-five or thirty years ago called Executive Women in Government. And there weren't many of us in policy-making positions. And I was then working for Virginia Neuwirth—you know, with the

White House. We helped to start this organization that is still thriving. And the idea was, give women a chance across government to network, because that is necessary with so few women in policy positions, and then help younger women coming along who wanted to follow our footsteps into government service. Show them some of the pitfalls along the way. Show them some shortcuts. Just give them the benefit of our experience. Margaret Chase Smith actually did that for me when I was twenty-two years old, just out of college. And she didn't know me from Adam. And she said, "I think you need to have some graduate work." And she encouraged me to go to law school.

That's terrific. And you went to Harvard? And you graduated in sixty-five?

My class was—this was still typical—24 women out of 550. And the first words I heard in that law school from a male classmate, the very first words: "Elizabeth, what are you doing here? What are you doing in this law school? Don't you realize there are men who would give their right arm to be here? Men who would use their legal education."

Oh, brother!

It was like throwing cold water in my face. Oh, we had Ladies' Day when the professor told—one time out of the whole semester—the five women in contracts class would have to write a poem. Sit in the front of the room and deliver their poem. And then he would ask questions.

This was at Harvard?

This was Harvard Law School. Professor Leach's Ladies' Day.

How revolting.

I know. The women wouldn't stand for it today. But we did.

Senator *Mary Landrieu*

DEMOCRAT FROM LOUISIANA

HT: Do you think that male senators treat women senators differently because there are more of you? And times have changed—the culture.

ML: The great news is that I think we are treated the same as our male colleagues, and that is a testament to the progress that has been made over the last several years. Because it wasn't always the case.

Patronized?

Oh, we were patronized. We were not taken seriously.

But a great deal has changed over the last twenty or thirty years. When I first got to the Louisiana Legislature in 1979, I wouldn't have answered that question in this way. There was a tremendous amount of discrimination. I was one of three women in the House of Representatives. I was twenty-three years old. So, besides being female, I was young and I was single. Most people were male, married, and older. And so there was—

They thought you were the intruder.

They thought I was an intruder. "What is she doing here?" The place was very unwelcoming.

I think women still have to—when they show themselves to be leaders—have to conform to a male model of leadership. And they are somewhat discouraged from being maybe their normal or regular self because it is not as accepted.

Sometimes, if a woman doesn't come across as very fierce or very strong, she is perceived to be weak—when the fact is she could be a very good leader, she just has a different style. So there are still some institutional biases.

And yet if she is very aggressive—

If she is very aggressive, then she is too aggressive.

How about your private life? Can you separate it out from all of your obligations?

I think this is a very important point for women who would think about a public career—to say that yes, you can separate your public life from your private life to a certain degree. In the sense that my husband and I, who are raising two small children—relatively, seven and eleven years old—have had a strong control of the schedule and that I only work a certain few nights a week. I am home with the children and the family the rest of the week. But this is a challenge to any parent, whether you are a mother or a father—to manage your schedule in a way that gives your family the time that they need and they deserve.

Now, in terms of being able to turn off work, it is not easy for anybody who has a very high level of responsibility to turn their work off.

Our job is not a nine-to-five job. It's pretty much twenty-four hours, seven days a week. But I do try on the weekends not to think too much about work. I really minimize the time that I watch TV—and, frankly, read the paper— because all it does is make me work. And I've got to go to soccer games and literally bake cookies and cook dinner. And I also travel home to the state regularly three times a month. But it helps me to have my family with me—my children and my husband with me. And fortunately my husband was willing to relocate to Washington.

And what impressions and messages would you like the people who visit this exhibit for women senators to take away with them?

Just how extraordinary the opportunity is for women in America to serve. And to say that our involvement in government is not necessarily the fruits of a strong democracy, but the legal status of women is really the seed that allows democracy to grow and flourish.

And I hope that this exhibit will encourage women to understand, not just individually what they can do themselves and what they might contribute themselves, but how important it is for women generally to have their status established legally in the law, because it really will help any country to grow and prosper.

Senator *Blanche Lincoln*

DEMOCRAT FROM ARKANSAS

HT: *Do you feel that people expect you to deal a lot with women's issues? And do women come to you—even beyond your constituency?*

BL: I think people do expect women legislators to have a different perspective, particularly on some of the things that have become known as women's issues—whether they be equality or whether they be family issues, children's issues—and I don't have a problem with that. I think it is important for us as women because it did take us longer to get the right to vote, and it has certainly taken us longer to be represented in our body of government. That we as women take on that responsibility and really work towards making sure that we bring about that equality.

But I also think that we have done a great job, as we have been here trying to point out to people and those that do want to qualify us as only being able to deal with women's issues—that women's issues are everything. And that women have a role to play, just as Senator Olympia Snowe and I have proven on the Finance Committee—women have a tremendous role to play in taxes and trade.

I don't know about you, but in our household I pay the bills. And when I was growing up, my mother did the books and she paid the bills. It was just a role that we play, I suppose. But I definitely think from the evolution of women in running the household, there is a tendency for women to be a little bit more practical when it comes to money matters. They are a little bit more conservative. When you talk about debt, women are a little bit more reluctant to get into debt.

Well, do you find that the male senators—are they still in that mood, "Oh you're so lucky to be here"?

We, as women, we really—in approaching the men from the correct perspective—when we come to the table, we demand respect because we have done our homework and we are willing to fight the fight. We are willing to do the battles that are necessary for the right reasons.

I come to the table and I give them the statistics of my state and the people that I represent. I tell them what I want to do and how I want to do it, having done my homework. And it's hard for them to argue with that or to patronize me, if I am actually standing up for the people who have sent me. Part of our responsibility as women and elected officials is to do the hard work that it takes in order to prove to people that women can do the job.

How do you respond to issues of personal image that seem to be in the questions raised in media on your hair, your dress, your style?

Oh, you absolutely get that criticism, and certainly you know that people are noticing that. I never will forget my first election. We were in a debate and of course the gentlemen had on their jackets. They took them off and rolled up their shirt sleeves, but they could not pay attention to what I had to say because I had a run in my panty hose.

People were fixated on that?

Well, it is just unbelievable. For women, I think there is no doubt the bar is higher in terms of your personal appearance. I don't take offense at that. As a woman from the South, I can remember one of my family members calling—I was on TV one time, and they said, "Somebody tell her to put some lipstick on."

How do you maintain private relationships? Family life and your work life and so forth.

I think if you recognize that there are multiple things that you want to accomplish and you want to be a success at all of them, you realize that you have to make choices at certain times. And the key is making sure that you make those correct choices—and that you don't put all of your eggs into a work basket and forget that family is very important. It is also important that family understands the responsibility that each of us has in terms of our service and what we are giving back, whether it is through our job or whether it is through our service.

Senator Lisa Murkowski
REPUBLICAN FROM ALASKA

LM: If you had suggested that I would be in the United States Senate a year ago—if you had made that suggestion, I would have told you that you were crazy, that I had my family to raise, that I had a perfectly good life.

HT: Did you have no stepping-stones into political life?

I have been in the state legislature for the past four years and I had just run for my third term and been elected—was selected by my colleagues in the Republican majority to be House Majority Leader and then was appointed to this position. So I've got that state legislative experience.

Of all the things you have done in your life, which ones really stand out for you?

Truly my greatest accomplishments are the boys that I have. I mean, I have two handsome, delightful, strong boys—

Every senator has said her family—

I take great pride in making a great choice when it came to choosing my partner—my husband. And my husband is caring for our two boys—we call him the Mr. Mom. And it is a good thing. It's very good for my boys, because I think that they are being raised in a household where there are no stereotypical roles in terms of who provides, who raises—there is a real sharing of that.

That's great. Are they in Alaska?

They are in Alaska. To make the decision to say, "I support you enough in what you are doing to take on the role of not only being Dad but Mom and taxi driver and nurse and all that goes with it"—and still run his business and accept what I am doing—it takes a pretty strong person.

Do you think that it is important for the women senators to get together? I think you get together about once a month and share a lot across party lines.

Yes. It's something that we all look forward to. It's important for me particularly, as a newcomer to the Senate and to the process, to know how other women handle it. I look at some of my male colleagues. I look at the example that my father set when he was in this role. And I can tell you, he was able to do a lot of what he did because my mother was in the background just providing that support. And most of us women here, either our husbands aren't here to provide that supportive spouse role or there are some that do not have a spouse—they don't have that relationship. And so it is different for us. And I think we will acknowledge that it is probably more lonely as a woman in the United States Senate. And yet, there's fourteen of us—I can't imagine what it was like when Barbara Mikulski was back here with just one other woman. And that wasn't too many years ago.

Senator *Patty Murray*

DEMOCRAT FROM WASHINGTON

HT: Does it make a difference being a woman in any sense of the word?

PM: I think it does today because I think people count on women to see things maybe differently, to try to find solutions, to work towards compromise, and to speak from a different side of their heart than oftentimes you see men do.

And do you think that has had an impact to have fourteen women in the Senate?

I do. We are on almost every single committee I think now in the Senate. I remember when I first came here, and there were a number of Senate committees that didn't have any women on there. And does it make a difference in committee? There is no doubt about it. I can give you a hundred different stories of where I was sitting there listening to a conversation on a committee and wondering when somebody is going to bring up some side of the issue. And then realizing there is no one else in this room that has ever lived that side of the issue, and I need to speak to it.

Do you think there will be more women in the Senate? Will it be a growing population?

I believe so. I think we went from two, who were in the Senate before I came in 1992, to now we are at fourteen. I think we will see more women elected in the coming year, and I have a theory on that. But I think we may taper off for a while, because opportunities for women are growing in a lot of different fields right now. So I think women have a lot of options to look at right now, and politics is a tough life and a tough row to hoe and they may not choose it as much, so we may level off for a while. But I think circumstances in the world and the country today really are a place where women are saying I need to get in and get involved in this.

Would you like to run for president?

No. I love what I do, I really do. I get to go out on the floor of the Senate and fight for things I care about. I was out on the floor today, I've been working on banning asbestos in this country for three years now. I have worked so closely with people who aren't here any more because they've died of mesothelioma. And to go out on the floor and be able to voice the words that they would voice had they been given the opportunity, it is such an honor to do that.

Isn't a tough part putting the arm on people, fund raising? You probably don't have to do it personally . . .

Well, I think it is important that you do do it personally. You are asking people to invest in you. You are saying support me—I need your help because I want to fight for these issues that I care about. So you are asking for people to invest in you, and I do think that it is important that you ask them personally.

When I first ran for the school board several decades ago, I had no money; I was earning $23,000 a year. I had to raise money to print brochures, so I talked my husband into having a garage sale, and we actually lost money. I mean checks bounced, I gave stuff away, I just am not the type to sell my stuff. So I learned very early on that if you don't ask people to help you, you preclude yourself from being able to run and do what you want to do.

Are there certain challenges in your life that prepared you to be a senator?

I jokingly tell people I had the best experience ever. I was a pre-school teacher. And I learned how to deal with four-year-olds, who could be very vociferous, who could be very belligerent, and who could take a lot of your time. That is good training for the Senate. But I think the truthful answer to that is partly that, but really I think all my life experiences. Growing up in a family where my father had multiple sclerosis and had to quit work. And my mom was raising seven kids, had to go back to work and get skills. She had to go to a vocational program. I saw what health care did to my dad, who couldn't change health care systems and his premiums went skyrocketing and he limped into Medicare when he was sixty-five. Because I live in a country that believes in investing in education, all seven of us got Pell grants and student loans, all of us graduated from college. So it is my life experience. Knowing how the American dream is real when you have a country that supports individuals is I think probably the best experience I had coming here.

And do you find that senators, male senators, treat you differently? I mean is there a sort of gap there?

I find it comes from both ends of the spectrum. In a way they are very sensitive to listening to women, because there aren't very many of us, and they know darn good and well that 50 percent of their voters at home are women. So our voices are listened to. But on the other hand, I think we all suffer from what women do in most professional fields, where you have to say it five times before they actually hear you say it. So we have to learn to keep repeating ourselves and taking credit for what we do.

Would you like to be a leader in the Senate? There hasn't been a woman majority leader yet.

You know, I've never thought about that. I do feel like I come to work every day and advocate for the people in my state and the issues I believe in. And in any way that I can perform those duties that makes life better for families like mine across the country, that is a good thing.

Is your husband a Democrat?

Of course he is. He is good Democrat. And he is actually really good for me, because he is out in the state and has his own job and sees life from a perspective that I don't see all the time. People say things to him, so he is kind of keeping my base real. And I'll tell you, my husband reminds me all the time who the constituents are that I am here for. When I was elected to the Senate, the night before the election, he said he was going to take me out to dinner. And he took me to Denny's. I was like what are you doing? He said I want you to look around this room, because if you win tomorrow, these are the people that you need to remember.

Senator *Maria Cantwell*

HT: How optimistic are you about the future of women being elected to the Senate?

MC: I come from a state where 50 percent of our legislators are women. And when I was in the state legislature about 25 percent were women. So in about a ten-to-fifteen-year period of time, we were able to double that. And I think that there are certain regions of the country that have shown a propensity, because I think women represent change, and I think that will continue as a trend.

How do you respond to issues of personal image that seem to be largely the province of women? Questions raised by the media or individuals about hair, dress, style?

I think it is unfortunate. I had a press person chase me down the hall one day saying, "Senator Cantwell, Senator Cantwell, I need to ask you a question." I turn around: "Yes?" "What do you think about Hillary's hair?" So you realize that people become obsessed with these issues, and it is unfortunate.

How do you maintain private relationships, romantic, family, and so forth? Do you have time for that?

Yes, but it is hard; you have to make it a priority. Living on two coasts makes it extra challenging. And

you have to find people who are empathetic with that schedule. It makes it really hard.

Is every social occasion a work obligation or are you able to have a social life where you can just kick off your shoes and relax?

Yes, I do that. And I just find that you have to be a person too. I've gone to several events in Seattle, and I think people think you should go work the room. I am like, no, I am here to have fun, I am here to enjoy the event. I'll say hi to people and I'll talk to people, but I don't think I have to go work the room.

So are there certain events, challenges, that you could point to in your life that prepared you to be in the Senate?

Lots of events. Well, I think my family was involved and interested in politics. My father had been on the city council in the Midwest. And our kitchen table was kind of the place where people came to talk to him about problems. He was definitely a rabble-rouser and took on the establishment. So I learned from that that you have to stand up for people.

So did you gear your life toward running for public office? Or politics?

No. I think I was always interested in politics, but I didn't think necessarily that I would run for office. But after moving to the Northwest, I got involved in building a library. I see something that really bugs me and then I get motivated. But in this case, the library had basically a leaking roof and they had water on the books. They had big problems, and they had tried to pass this library bond a couple of times to build a new library. And it had failed, so I took on this effort to pass it. So it was that that got me going and I said, well, maybe there are other things here I should be involved with.

And you found out you could do things.
Yes.
Even though you don't achieve it the first day you try or even whole weeks later.
Yes, I think that is the key thing for me, and it has been, is that persistence usually pays off.
Do you think we'll have a woman president early in this century, and would you like to run?
I have no interest in running for president, but I think it is important that we do get a woman to be president in the early part of this century. And the reason I say that is that I just think that women do represent agents of change and a different perspective, and I think it is time to have that kind of feminine power in the White House.
Do you think a woman president would be different, would act differently?
I think that we call on different things. I think it is a great source of strength and I think that it would be a great time to have a woman leader.
But do you think women are more sympathetic to the human problems?

I think that the feminine side has a center and a core that drives us. I think that it drives us to be concerned about those things. I had this interesting experience, and it is one of the legislative things I am most proud of. I passed what was our state's growth management law, I think it was the early nineties, like 1991. And we had rapid growth and big problems with transportation. Any way, the Speaker of the House said I am going to appoint these six committee chairs to work together, because this bill has jurisdiction in various committees. I am going to appoint the chairman of the local government committee, the transportation committee, the natural resources committee, the environment committee, the trade and economic development committee, the housing committee. And I want all of you people to work together and not get into turf battles about your jurisdiction and come up with this landmark legislation that is needed at this time. It turned out that all the chairmen of those committees were women.
You're kidding, impossible.
Exactly. And I think it a little bit freaked the guys out at first, because they were like, they called us the Steel Magnolias, because that was when that movie came out. But I have thought about that a thousand times, that I don't really think we would have gotten that legislation, which was landmark legislation, if those six committee chairmen had been men. I don't think we all would have said, okay, I'll give up my jurisdiction on that, or okay, I'll do that.

Senator *Olympia Snowe*

REPUBLICAN FROM MAINE

HT: You are not the typical Republican these days. Is it still the old boys' club in the Senate?

OS: I think less so. I think because, obviously, there is a greater preponderance of women's voices in the United States Senate. I think it is very different from what the institution used to be, and I can only imagine what it would have been like when there were only one or two women. I think now with more women's voices in the Senate, it has certainly changed the tenor and I think the whole character of the Senate. I remember seeing a former senator, last year in the cloak room. And he had served here back in the seventies, and I said what looks different to you in the Senate, and he said, seeing so many women. Interesting when you think about it, that is the one thing that became apparent to him, that there were women serving in the United States Senate, so it clearly has changed.

Do you think your male colleagues patronize you or are like, there, there, little girl?

No, I think that a lot has changed. Now I don't hear what they are saying behind my back, but I think they truly understand the role we play and respect the role. Everybody does their homework.

Are you interested in running for president?

Well, that would be a shocker in my party, a pro-choice Republican. That would reverberate. So it is not likely that I will, but I do think that . . .

But that isn't what is keeping you from running. Would you care about running?

But I think it would be an interesting challenge. There is no question, I mean it is very different being the chief executive, being the president of the United States, as opposed to being in the legislative branch as I've been for thirty years. So I can see the fascination and attraction for being the president of the United States; it is a totally different perspective. But it is not something that I am certainly planning on. But I do fully expect that a woman will be president in the near future. I think women should run. I don't think there should be hesitancy, and I think the American people would be prepared, for the right candidate.

You think at this point?

Yes, I do, I really do. I think if the right person runs, in the sense that person responds and resonates with the American people. If it is the right timing for that particular individual, given that person's views, and speaking to the issues that people are concerned about at that moment in time, I don't think the people of this country would hesitate whatsoever. It is just having the right background, the right depth and breadth, the right connection to the American people.

Do you find any obstacles in your own life, I mean in dividing up your time with your personal life?

No, because my husband is fortunately as busy as I am. He has a very major responsibility; he owns a public company. And lots of people say, when do you get to see each other, which is a logical question. We both travel. It is weekends. But we have finally agreed that we are so busy during the week, we wouldn't have a chance to see each other anyway. So it gives us time to focus on our work, and we get to see each other . . .

. . . you go home every weekend?

Just about every weekend or he comes here. Or I travel to Maine and that is where we meet. But it is trying to fuse those responsibilities. And also at a time when people are commuting to their jobs, so it is not so unusual now for couples to live this kind of life. It is not atypical anymore, but I see more women I think using the political avenues. I think that is very healthy for the political system; it is healthy for America, healthy for this institution, to have a women's voice be a part of the political process and the decisions that are made.

Are there any issues like that now, where women are pushing?

We've done a number of issues together, obviously the health issues, like breast cancer and mammograms. Genetic testing is an issue that I have been working on for quite some time, that just passed the United States Senate. We also got together about the plight of women and children of Afghanistan and the aftermath of the Taliban.

Having women represented in the political process can make all the difference on some of these issues. On welfare reform, Senator Blanche Lincoln and I serve on the Finance Committee. We worked on a number of issues across the political aisle on the committee in 2001. We worked on child tax credits, and I spearheaded the refundable child tax credits; she was a great ally in that respect. It is the voices of women that have prevailed and made all the difference for women in a working environment.

Has your life changed since 9/11?

That is an interesting question. Not personally, but I think certainly my capacities as a United States senator . . . you feel a greater responsibility for the security of the United States. I think it brought that home, the enormity of the challenge we face and how sensitive we now are to the idea of having terrorism within our boundaries.

Senator *Susan Collins*

REPUBLICAN FROM MAINE

HT: Do you aspire to any higher office, president for example?

SC: I am glad to hear that. I am not one who envisions herself running for president some day. I am very happy in the Senate. I feel like I make a real difference every day. I do think that many of my colleagues in the Senate would be outstanding as president or as presidential candidates. But if I had to predict, I bet that the first woman president will have been a governor.

Why is that?

Because governor is an executive position. And I think that if you show you can run a state, the voters are likely to feel more comfortable with you running the country. I will never forget, when I ran unsuccessfully for governor of Maine, a young banker saying to me that he agreed with all my positions on the issues, but he just couldn't imagine a woman running the state of Maine. I was so shocked to realize that that glass ceiling for executive positions still existed.

And do you have friends on the other side of the fence?

I do indeed. I frequently team up, for example, with Maria Cantwell on a lot of job training issues that affect our states. I have worked with Dianne Feinstein on cancer research issues.

And you all get together once a month or so?

It is about once a month. We have a wonderful time because the bonds you have as women senators transcend party and geography and ideology. If you have run for federal office as a woman, you have a bond.

Do you adjust how you look and your hair and everything by what your friends say or do you feel compelled to look a certain way when you go to work?

I feel that I should look professional every day. Where it does become an issue is when I am home in Bangor, in Maine, where I live, and I need to do a quick errand. And I've learned the hard way that I can't just rush out in my sweatsuit with no makeup.

There might be a camera ready . . .

Exactly. That actually happened to me one Christmas time. I was doing some last-minute mailing of Christmas presents, and I thought, I don't have time to change. So I went out in a sweatsuit with no makeup on, and sure enough, down at the post office was the television crew that was doing a story on people who waited 'til the last minute to mail their Christmas presents. And you can imagine who they wanted to interview.

In terms of your social life, do you feel when you go out socially, a reception or dinner, that you are always on in the sense that you have to be the senator?

This job is all-consuming, and it does take a great deal of one's personal time, but I think that is true for both men and women who serve in the Senate. The demands are enormous, and a lot of what may appear to be social occasions really are not. But nevertheless, when I am home in Maine, I still find it possible in the summer to go kayaking and to just relax.

Women in the Senate, 1789–2005: Routes to Office
CENTER FOR AMERICAN WOMEN AND POLITICS

I N the earliest years after women won the vote, women often entered Congress by succeeding their husbands. More recently, women have built their own political careers, often first holding office at the local or state level. Sixteen, or 48 percent, of all women who have served in the Senate held previous elective office. In 2003, ten (77 percent) of the women serving in the Senate had previously held elective office. Of the thirty-three women who have served in the Senate, fifteen have entered through regular election, thirteen entered by an appointment to an unexpired term, and five succeeded to the unexpired term through a special election.

It took 133 years for the first woman to serve in the U.S. Senate. Rebecca Latimer Felton was appointed in 1922 to serve in the Senate.

Rebecca Latimer Felton (D-GA)
Senate Term: 11/21/22–11/22/22
Educator, writer, lecturer, and reformer. The first woman to serve in the United States Senate, she took the oath of office on November 21, 1922. Having been appointed to fill a vacancy, Felton served for just two days.

Hattie Wyatt Caraway (D-AR)
Senate Term: 12/8/31–1/2/45
Appointed to fill vacancy caused by death of her husband; later elected to complete his term and subsequently to two full terms before losing bid for reelection. Chairwoman, Committee on Enrolled Bills.

Rose McConnell Long (D-LA)
Senate Term: 2/10/36–1/2/37
Appointed and subsequently elected to fill vacancy caused by death of husband.

Dixie Bibb Graves (D-AL)
Senate Term: 8/20/37–1/10/38
Civic leader and activist. Appointed by husband (who was governor) to fill vacancy caused by resignation. Resigned when a successor was appointed.

Gladys Pyle (R-SD)
Senate Term: 11/9/38–1/3/39
State legislator and secretary of state; ran for governor in 1930. Elected to fill vacancy caused by death. Never sworn in because Congress was not in session.

Vera Cahalan Bushfield (R-SD)
Senate Term: 10/6/48–12/27/48
Appointed to fill vacancy caused by death of her husband, but did not take seat because Congress was not in session; resigned when successor was elected.

Margaret Chase Smith (R-ME)
Senate Term: 1/3/49–1/3/73
Businesswoman and congressional aide. Elected to House of Representatives to fill vacancy caused by death of husband; served four full terms, then elected to four full terms in Senate; lost bid for re-election.

Margaret Chase Smith was the first woman to be elected to the Senate without having first been appointed to serve.

Eva Kelley Bowring (R-NE)
Senate Term: 4/26/54–11/7/54
Rancher and party activist. Appointed to fill vacancy caused by death of Dwight Griswold; served until Hazel Hempel Abel was elected to complete term.

Hazel Hempel Abel (R-NE)
Senate Term: 11/8/54–12/31/54
Educator, businesswoman, and party activist. Elected to fill vacancy caused by death of Dwight Griswold; resigned when successor was elected.

Maurine Brown Neuberger (D-OR)
Senate Term: 11/8/60–1/3/67
Educator, state legislator, writer, and lecturer. Elected to fill vacancy caused by death of husband; simultaneously elected for ensuing full term.

Elaine S. Edwards (D-LA)
Senate Term: 8/7/72–11/13/72
Appointed by husband (who was governor) to fill vacancy caused by death; resigned when successor was appointed.

Muriel Humphrey (D-MN)
Senate Term: 2/6/78–11/7/78
Appointed to fill vacancy caused by death of her husband; resigned when successor was elected.

Maryon Pittman Allen (D-AL)

Senate Term: 6/12/78–11/7/78

Journalist, educator, writer, and lecturer. Appointed to fill vacancy caused by death of her husband; lost bid for re-nomination and resigned when her successor was elected.

Nancy Landon Kassebaum (R-KS)

Senate Term: 12/23/78–1/7/97

Maize School Board member, congressional aide, and radio station executive. Won general election, then appointed to fill vacancy caused by resignation; won two subsequent terms in 1984 and 1990. Chaired Senate Committee on Labor and Human Resources in 104th Congress. Retired.

Paula Hawkins (R-FL)

Senate Term: 1/1/81-1/3/87

Businesswoman and public service commissioner. Won general election, then appointed to fill vacancy caused by resignation of predecessor; lost bid for re-election.

Barbara Mikulski (D-MD)

Senate Term: 1/3/87–present

U.S. representative; social worker; Baltimore city council member. Won general election after serving five terms in U.S. House of Representatives. Re-elected in 1992, 1998, and 2004.

Jocelyn Birch Burdick (D-ND)

Senate Term: 9/16/92–12/14/92

Civic activist. Appointed to fill vacancy caused by death of her husband. Resigned when successor was chosen in special election.

Dianne Feinstein (D-CA)

Senate Term: 11/10/92–present

San Francisco mayor and San Francisco Board of Supervisors member and president. Ran unsuccessfully for governor in 1990. Won special election to fill vacancy caused by resignation; seat had been filled temporarily by appointee. Won terms in 1994 and in 2000.

Barbara Boxer (D-CA)

Senate Term: 1/5/93–present

U.S. representative, Marin County Board of Supervisors member and president, stockbroker, and journalist. Won open seat in general election after five terms in U.S. House of Representatives. Re-elected in 1998 and 2004.

Carol Moseley Braun (D-IL)

Senate Term: 1/5/93–1/6/99

Attorney, Cook County Recorder of Deeds, and state representative. Defeated incumbent in primary and went on to win open seat in general election. Lost re-election bid in 1998.

Nancy Landon Kassebaum was the first woman to be elected in her own right without having previously filled an unexpired Congressional term. She was the first woman to chair a major committee, the Committee on Labor and Human Resources in the 104th Congress.

Carol Moseley Braun was the first African American woman to serve in the Senate and the only woman of color to date.

Patty Murray (D-WA)

Senate Term: 1/5/93–present
State senator, citizen lobbyist. Won open seat in general election. Re-elected in 1998 and 2004.

Kay Bailey Hutchison (R-TX)

Senate Term: 6/14/93–present
State treasurer, businesswoman, state representative, TV newscaster, attorney. Won special election to fill vacancy caused by resignation; seat had been filled temporarily by appointee. Won full term in 1994 and 2000.

Olympia Jean Snowe (R-ME)

Senate Term: 1/4/95–present
U.S. representative, state senator and state representative, member of Auburn Board of Voter Registration. Won open seat in general election after serving eight terms in U.S. House. Re-elected in 2000.

Olympia Snowe was the first woman, and the only Republican woman to date, to be elected to her state house, state senate, the U.S. House, and the U.S. Senate.

Sheila Frahm (R-KS)

Senate Term: 6/11/96–11/8/96
Lieutenant governor and secretary of administration, state senator and senate majority leader, State Board of Education member and vice chair, Colby School Board member, farmer. Appointed to fill vacancy caused by resignation, lost primary bid.

Susan Collins (R-ME)

Senate Term: 1/7/97–present
Businesswoman, regional Small Business Administration Administrator, state cabinet member. Won open seat in general election.

Mary Landrieu (D-LA)

Senate Term: 1/7/97–present
State treasurer, state representative, unsuccessful candidate for governor in 1995. Won open seat in general election in 1996 and re-election after a runoff in 2002.

Blanche Lincoln (D-AR)

Senate Term: 1/6/99–present
U.S. representative; congressional staff member; legislative affairs specialist. Won open seat in the general election of 1998.

Maria E. Cantwell (D-WA)

Senate Term: 1/3/01–present
U.S. representative; state representative; technology executive. Defeated incumbent by narrow margin to make Washington 4th state to send two women to the U.S. Senate simultaneously.

Jean Carnahan (D-MO)

Senate Term: 1/3/01–11/23/02
Children's advocate; author. Appointed to a two-year term to fill her husband's seat after he was elected posthumously. Lost bid for re-election in 2002.

Hillary Rodham Clinton (D-NY)

Senate Term: 1/3/01–present

Only First Lady elected to public office; first woman from New York elected to the U.S. Senate; attorney; author; children's advocate. Won open seat in general election.

Deborah Stabenow (D-MI)

Senate Term: 1/3/01–present

U.S. representative; state senator; state representative; first woman chair of Ingham County Board of Commissioners; social worker. Defeated incumbent to become first woman from Michigan elected to U.S. Senate.

Lisa Murkowski (R-AK)

Senate Term: 12/20/02–present

State house majority leader; state representative; state Republican committeewoman; community activist; attorney. Appointed by her father to fill vacancy created when he resigned to become governor.

Elizabeth Dole (R-NC)

Senate Term: 1/7/03–present

Presidential candidate; presidential cabinet member and staff member; federal trade commissioner; president of the American Red Cross. Won open seat in general election 2002.

Women in the Senate: Do They Make a Difference?

CENTER FOR AMERICAN WOMEN AND POLITICS

S INCE the Center for American Women and Politics (CAWP) began tracking women's status and progress in electoral office in 1971, the overall pattern has been slow, incremental change punctuated by occasional momentous change. The elections of 1992 and 2000 were watershed years for women's representation in the U.S. Senate. Four of the five members elected in 1992 are still serving, and four additional women joined them in 2000. But as of 2004, the numbers of women officeholders at most levels of office seem stagnant, except at the gubernatorial level, where nine women currently serve, up significantly from five in 2002.

Why do we care how many women represent us at any level of office? CAWP's research on women state legislators shows that women lawmakers make a difference; they refocus the policy agenda, open up institutional processes, and provide access to previously marginalized groups. Research has shown that women in Congress, as a group, also differ from their male colleagues in two important ways: the policies they promote and the ways they work. These differences—inevitably mediated by institutional forces, partisanship, and the political climate—resemble differences found between men and women in state legislatures.

In particular, women in Congress say they have a special obligation to represent women, although each interprets that responsibility differently. Numerous sources (e.g., Dodson et. al., Rosenthal) report a recurring scenario described by many women in Congress: whether or not she originally envisioned herself as a voice for women, each recounts her discovery, upon arriving in Washington, that certain issues or perspectives were being addressed inadequately, if at all. If the Congresswomen did not speak up, these women realized, women's interests would be neglected.

Taking up the challenge, women have altered the Congressional agenda by highlighting new issues, framing policy concerns in distinctive ways, and expanding the terms of debate over legislation. Women's health concerns—including health care and research—are most frequently cited as areas where the presence of women in Congress has resulted in noticeably different policies. Welfare policy and reproductive rights have also been noted by researchers as areas where the distinctive impact of women lawmakers can be observed.

Recommended readings:

Burrell, Barbara C. *A Woman's Place Is in the House: Campaigning for Congress in the Feminist Era.* Ann Arbor: University of Michigan Press, 1994.

Carroll, Susan J. *The Impact of Women in Public Office.* Bloomington: Indiana University Press, 2001.

Casey, Kathleen J., and Susan J. Carroll. "Welfare Reform in the 104th Congress: Institutional Position and the Role of Women." In Nancy J. Hirschmann and Ulrike Liebert, eds., *Women and Welfare: Theory and Practice in the United States and Europe.* New Brunswick, NJ: Rutgers University Press, 2001.

Congressional Quarterly Inc. *CQ Women in Power Profiles from the 108th Congress.* Congressional Studies Series. Washington, D.C.: Congressional Quarterly Inc., 2002.

Dodson, Debra L., Susan J. Carroll, Ruth B. Mandel, Katherine E. Kleeman, Ronnee Schreiber, and Debra Liebowitz. *Voices, Views, Votes: The Impact of Women in the 103rd Congress.* New Brunswick, NJ: Center for American Women and Politics, 1995.

Fox, Richard I. *Gender Dynamics in Congressional Elections.* Thousand Oaks: Sage Publications, 1997.

Gertzog, Irwin N. *Women and Power on Capitol Hill: Reconstructing the Congressional Women's Caucus.* Boulder: Lynne Rienner Publishers, 2004.

Hawkesworth, Mary, Debra Dodson, Katherine E. Kleeman, Kathleen J. Casey, and Krista Jenkins. *Legislating By and For Women: A Comparison of the 103rd and 104th Congresses.* New Brunswick, NJ: Center for American Women and Politics, 2001.

Mikulski, Barbara, et. al. *Nine and Counting: The Women of the Senate.* New York: HarperCollins Books, 2000.

O'Connor, Karen. *Women and Congress: Running, Winning, and Ruling.* New York: Haworth Press, 2001.

Rosenthal, Cindy Simon, ed. *Women Transforming Congress.* Norman, OK: University of Oklahoma Press, 2002.

Sherman, Janann. *No Place for a Woman: The Life of Senator Margaret Chase Smith.* New Brunswick, NJ: Rutgers University Press, 2000.

Swers, Michele L. *The Difference Women Make: The Policy Impact of Women in Congress.* Chicago: University of Chicago Press, 2002.

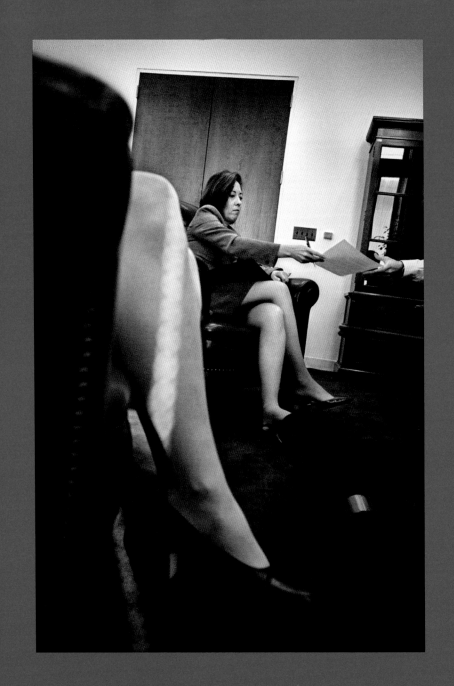

Women in Office

The Status of Women in Elective Office, 2005

Congress

IN 2005, women hold 80, or 15 percent, of the 535 seats in the 109th U.S. Congress—14, or 14 percent, of the 100 seats in the Senate and 66, or 15.2 percent, of the 435 seats in the House of Representatives. In addition, three women serve as Delegates to the House from Guam, the Virgin Islands, and Washington, D.C. Of the 80 women serving in Congress, 20, or 25 percent, are women of color;* in addition, an African American woman and a Caribbean American woman serve as Delegates to the House from Washington, D.C., and the Virgin Islands, respectively. Women of color constitute 3.7 percent of the total 535 members of Congress.

*We use "women of color" when referring to African American, Asian American/Pacific Islander, Caribbean American, Latina, and Native American women as a group. We understand that both the terms "women of color" and "minority women" are problematic, but know of no preferable inclusive term.

Fourteen women serve in the Senate: Barbara Boxer (D-CA), Maria Cantwell (D-WA), Hillary Rodham Clinton (D-NY), Susan Collins (R-ME), Elizabeth Dole (R-NC), Dianne Feinstein (D-CA), Kay Bailey Hutchison (R-TX), Mary Landrieu (D-LA), Blanche Lincoln (D-AR), Barbara Mikulski (D-MD), Lisa Murkowski (R-AK), Patty Murray (D-WA), Olympia Snowe (R-ME), and Debbie Stabenow (D-MI).

Sixty-six women from 26 states serve in the House of Representatives; 43 are Democrats and 23 are Republicans. In addition, three Democratic women serve as the Delegates to the House from Guam, the Virgin Islands, and Washington, D.C.

Statewide Elective Executive

In 2005, 80 women hold statewide elective executive offices across the country; women hold 25.4 percent of the 315 available positions. Among these women, 34 are Democrats, 43 are Republicans, and 3 were elected in nonpartisan races. Of the women serving in statewide elective executive offices, 5, or 6.3 percent, are women of color. Women of color constitute 1.6 percent of the total 315 statewide elective executives.

State Legislatures

In 2005, 1,664, or 22.5 percent, of the 7,382 state legislators in the United States are women. Women hold 400, or 20.3 percent, of the 1,971 state senate seats and 1,264, or 23.4 percent, of the 5,411 state house seats. The number of women serving in state legislatures has increased more than fivefold since 1969, when 301, or 4.0 percent, of all state legislators were women. Of the women state legislators serving nationwide, 316 or 19 percent are women of color. They include 84 senators and 232 representatives; all but 19 are Democrats. Women of color constitute 4.3 percent of the total 7,382 state legislators.

The Ten States with the Highest Percentages of Women State Legislators

STATE	% WOMEN	STATE	% WOMEN
Maryland	34.0	Washington	33.3
Delaware	33.9	Colorado	33.0
Arizona	33.3	Kansas	32.7
Nevada	33.3	New Mexico	31.3
Vermont	33.3	California	30.8

Afterword

BY MELINA MARA

I was seven years old when my Uncle Dick asked me what I wanted to be when I grew up. I didn't hesitate. "President of the United States," I said. Everyone laughed—except my mother. Like many of the other strong women who shaped my life, she believed I could be whatever I wanted.

The year was 1969, the early days of a movement that would redefine women's work and women's place in society.

But years later, when I was majoring in political science at Sarah Lawrence College, there were still only two women in the most powerful club in the country: the U.S. Senate.

It wasn't until 1998, when I was working on a story about Washington State Senator Patty Murray, that I realized the balance had suddenly shifted. There were now nine women senators.

Some of the press responded with a flurry of lifestyles stories: Senator Maria Cantwell and her mother baking cookies; Senator Susan Collins kayaking in Maine.

This project grew out of my desire to go beyond the fluff and document this moment in history. My goal was to show these women doing the hard work of government.

For a photographer, the hard work was to get beyond the spin and the contrived photo ops to the real people. I spent three years shadowing the women as much as they would tolerate, and as much as my meager budget would allow. Sometimes the senators let me behind the scenes while they worked the phones, met with staff, and brokered deals. At other times, I followed them through their public rounds. Always, I tried to find a real moment in the midst of the staged news events, the whisper between colleagues, the gesture that truly tells the story.

When the exhibit went on display, I discovered that the story I set out to tell wasn't always the one the viewer saw.

The photograph of the diminutive Patty Murray flanked by towering men inspired very different reactions. One person said it made her look small, powerless. Many more felt as I did—that the image showed a woman holding her own in our country's corridors of power.

One of my favorite pictures in the book was, like many others, a result of luck and bucking authority.

It was the first anniversary of the September 11 attacks. All of the senators were lining up outside for a ceremony. Normally, I would have approached the scene from the front. But security restrictions required the press to enter from the back door the senators used. Because of that, I saw what the audience didn't: Senator Kay Bailey Hutchison retrieving her daughter, Bailey, who preferred to play in a fountain instead of standing in a line of politicians.

As I was shooting, a security guard grabbed my arm and told me to stop. Another threatened to confiscate my film. I kept taking pictures, then convinced them not to take my film. The result was the signature photo for the exhibit. It shows a woman juggling the roles of lawmaker and mother.

Our grandmothers might never have imagined it. But women like my mother always knew it would happen someday.

Acknowledgments

This project's completion was a long shot from the beginning. But there are certain people and organizations that made my idea and then my work a reality. A gathering of collaborators, advisors, people at the top of their field, family and friends formed into a team around me, and without them I would have not been successful.

A special thanks to Ellen Malcolm and the Windom Fund. Without her funding and support of this work I wouldn't have gotten very far. I will always remember the brief meeting where Ellen said that she would support the project: she looked at me and said, "Don't worry about money. Now go tell the story." I am probably not quoting her with absolute accuracy, but her words motivated and directed me.

This work came together in this form with the cooperation, understanding, and patience of several collaborators. We produced a multi-layered form that tells a richer story when all the layers are brought together. Veteran White House correspondent Helen Thomas added her voice and journalism to this project, thus expanding its depth and insight.

To the Center for American Women in Politics at Rutgers University, Debbie Walsh and Kathleen Casey, I owe a great debt. I thank them not only for their work within these pages, but for the friendship, hard work, scholarship, and facilitation involved in making such a project come together. Thank you to Don Carleton, an unwavering advocate for political photography, and the Center for American History at the University of Texas in Austin, and their staff and curator Lynn Bell; without their help there would be no book and no traveling exhibit. The project's team needs a special thank-you, to all the editors, designers, hanger/installers, curators, and friends who kept the work's standards high. The project's two photo editors, Janet Jensen and Casey Madison, broke me of my stubbornness after many discussions and battles, which allowed me to grow and the work to tell a better story.

And finally, thanks to the U.S. women senators and to the many who have shown great support for this project. On the opening night of the exhibit, a certain senator, after looking at the show, beckoned me over and said, "Now I understand." This story is about you, the fourteen women who hold positions of power never held before by so many women at one time, and your 24/7 commitment to these jobs. I thank you for the opportunity to document you at work and chronicle your historic impact on American government today.

Special thanks to my family: parents, grandparents, aunts, uncles, and wonderful cousins—and they know who they are in heaven and on earth—who encouraged me to take risks, break rules, and journey down my own path. My cousin Susan Mania was one of the exhibit hanger/installers for the Smithsonian show. She and her partner Christyl Cusworth created a template design for displaying the work, which all the other venues have emulated. On the exhibit's opening night at the Smithsonian, I was surrounded by the love of my cousins Lucille and Vinnie Marchitelli, George Spagnola, and my endlessly supportive aunt, Amelia Tuccillo. I am blessed by the love of my family.

Particular thanks to my extended family and friends whose constant support and talents were invaluable during this project. And to Janet Jensen, who edited, critiqued, labored, and pushed to maintain the high standards of this journalistic project. She patiently supported and gave of herself, and this project's success is greatly due to her work.

Specifically I would like to thank:

> The fourteen women U.S. senators and their staffs for giving me the opportunity to tell this story.

> Ellen Dorn and the Smithsonian Institution, for believing in the work and its need to be exhibited.

Project team

Sandra Eisert, contributing editor
Casey Madison, photo editor
Janet Jensen, photo editor
Helen Thomas, interviews
Kathleen Casey, Center for American Women and
    Politics: Eagleton Institute of Politics, Rutgers
    University, The State University of New Jersey
Amy Bain, Center for American Women and
    Politics: Eagleton Institute of Politics, Rutgers
    University, The State University of New Jersey
Christyl Cusworth, hanger/installer

Susan Mania, hanger/installer
Kate Feeley Agnew, liaison
Christine Patronik-Holder, communications
Don Marquis, photo editor, *Chicago Tribune*
Melissa Schiffman, audio recording
Emily Murphy, audio editor
Daniel Meijer, audio coordinator
Jeremy Harrison, production artist
Sara Herrett, Ivey Imaging
Jose Azel and Aurora/Quanta

Special thanks

Amelia Tuccillo
Elizabeth Feeley
Sarah Voisin
Jane Menyawi
Bill Auth
The (Tacoma) News Tribune Photo Staff and David
    Zeeck, managing editor
Scott Simon, National Public Radio
Debbie Walsh, Center for American Women and
    Politics: Eagleton Institute of Politics, Rutgers
    University, The State University of New Jersey
Don Carleton, The Center for American History
    University of Texas at Austin
Lynn Bell, The Center for American History
    University of Texas at Austin
P. F. Bentley, photographer

Joe Solmonese, EMILY's List
Lisa Robillard, EMILY's List
Pat Giardina Carpenter, WISH List
Florence Nash, editor
Hearst Newspapers
Cheryl Reed
Stephanie Simons
Sandi Doughton
Rick Manugian
Skip Card
Lui Kit Wong
Duncan Livingston
Russ Carmack
Leslie Burnbaum
Bill Stevens
Scott Oberstaller